KUMON MATH WORKBOOKS

Grade 1

P9-DMI-524

Addition

Table of Contents

KUMON

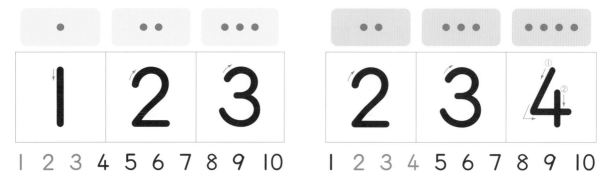

1 2 3 4 5 6 7 8 9 10

2 3 4 5 6 7 8 9 10

---

1 Trace the gray numbers from • to ★.

（1）

（2）

---

2 Trace the gray numbers from • to ★.

（1）

（2）

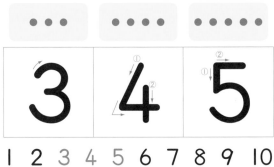

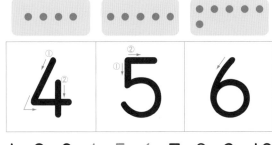

1 2 3 4 5 6 7 8 9 10   1 2 3 4 5 6 7 8 9 10

3 **Trace the gray numbers from • to ★.**

(1)

(2)

4 **Trace the gray numbers from • to ★.**

(1)

(2)

Let's trace the numbers and try to keep within the lines.

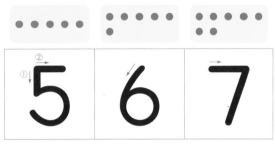

1 2 3 4 5 6 7 8 9 10   1 2 3 4 5 6 7 8 9 10

1 Trace the gray numbers from • to ★.

(1)   (2)

2 Trace the gray numbers from • to ★.

(1)   (2)

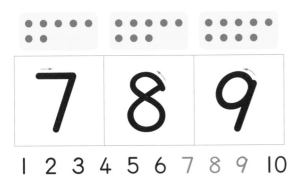

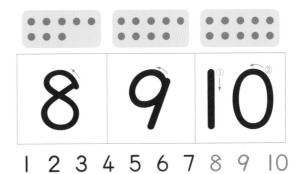

1 2 3 4 5 6 7 8 9 10   1 2 3 4 5 6 7 8 9 10

3 Trace the gray numbers from ● to ★.

(1)

(2)

4 Trace the gray numbers from ● to ★.

(1)

(2)

Are you keeping within the lines?
Good job!

5

1 Write each number while looking at the example above.

2 points per question

Example

| 1 | 2 | 3 | 4 | 5 |
| 6 | 7 | 8 | 9 | 10 |

2 How many dots are there? Write the numbers in each box.

3 points per question

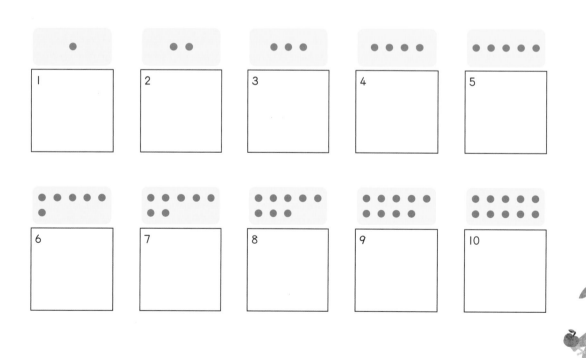

③ Write each number while looking at the example above.

2 points per question

Example

1	2	3	4	5
6	7	8	9	10

1	2	3	4	5
6	7	8	9	10

④ How many dots are there?
Write the numbers in each box.

3 points per question

  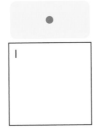  

3	4	1	2	0

There are no dots here. What does that mean?

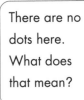

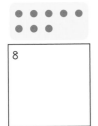 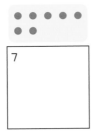 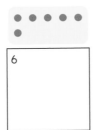 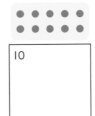 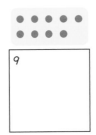

8	7	6	10	9

When you finish the exercises, let's check your answers with your parents.

4 Writing Numbers ◆1 to 15

Level ☆☆

Date / /

Name

Score /100

1 Write each number while looking at the example above.

2 points per question

Example

1	2	3	4	5
6	7	8	9	10

1	2			5
6			9	10

2 How many dots are there? Write the numbers in each box.

3 points per question

3	6	4		

There are no dots here. What does that mean?

3 Trace each gray number while looking at the example above.

3 points per question

Example

1	2	3	4	5
6	7	8	9	10
11	12	13	14	15

1	2	3	4	5
6	7	8	9	10
11	12	13	14	15

4 Fill in the missing numbers.

5 points per question

1	2	3	4	5
6	7	8	9	10
11	12	13	14	15

1	2	3	4	5
6	7	8	9	10
11	12	13	14	15

When you are done, check your answers by using the answer key in the back of this workbook!

5 Writing Numbers ◆ 1 to 20

Level ☆☆

Date / /

Name

Score /100

① Trace the gray numbers.

2 points per question

1	2	3	4	5
6	7	8	9	10
11	12	13	14	15
16	17	18	19	20

② Fill in the missing numbers.

3 points per question

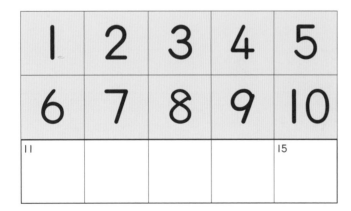

1	2	3	4	5
6	7	8	9	10
11				15

③ Fill in the missing numbers.

3 points per question

11	12	13	14	15
16				20

4 **Fill in the missing numbers.**

3 points per question

1	2	3	4	5
6	7	8	9	10
11	12	13	14	15
16				20

5 **Fill in the missing numbers.**

3 points per question

11	12	13	14	15
16				20

6 **Count the dots and fill in the missing numbers.**

3 points per question

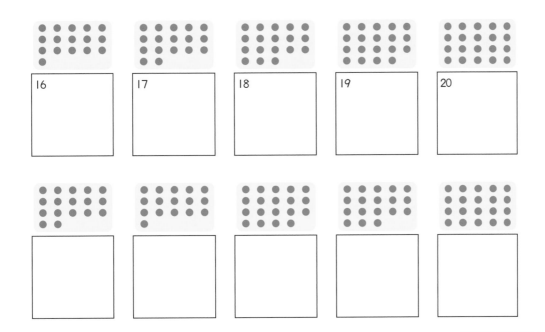

16	17	18	19	20

Did you remember all your numbers up to 20?

1 Trace the gray numbers and fill in the missing numbers.

2 points per question

1	2	3							10
1	2								
11	12	13	14	15	16	17	18	19	20
21	22	23	24	25	26	27	28	29	30

2 Fill in the missing numbers.

3 points per question

1	2	3	4	5	6	7	8	9	10
11	12								20
21	22	23	24	25	26	27	28	29	30

3 Fill in the missing numbers.

3 points per question

1	2	3	4	5	6	7	8	9	10
11	12								20
21	22	23	24	25	26	27	28	29	30

4 Trace the gray numbers.

2 points per question

1	2	3	4	5	6	7	8	9	10
11	12	13	14	15	16	17	18	19	20
21	22	23	24	25	26	27	28	29	30

Nice job! You can write all your numbers up to 30!

Date / /

Name

1 **Fill in the missing numbers.**

3 points per question

1	2	3	4	5	6	7	8	9	10
11	12	13	14	15	16	17	18	19	20
21	22							29	30

2 **Trace the gray numbers.**

2 points per question

1	2	3	4	5	6	7	8	9	10
11	12	13	14	15	16	17	18	19	20
21	22	23	24	25	26	27	28	29	30
31	32	33	34	35	36	37	38	39	40

3 Fill in the missing numbers.

3 points per question

1	2	3	4	5	6	7	8	9	10
11	12	13	14	15	16	17	18	19	20
21	22	23	24	25	26	27	28	29	30
31	32							39	40

4 Trace the gray numbers.

2 points per question

1	2	3	4	5	6	7	8	9	10
11	12	13	14	15	16	17	18	19	20
21	22	23	24	25	26	27	28	29	30
31	32	33	34	35	36	37	38	39	40
41	42	43	44	45	46	47	48	49	50

We're already at 50! Are you ready to count to 100?

8 Table of Numbers ◆ 1 to 100

Level ★★

Date / /

Name

Score /100

1 Fill in the missing numbers.

3 points per question

1	2	3	4	5	6	7	8	9	10
11	12	13	14	15	16	17	18	19	20
21	22	23	24	25	26	27	28	29	30
31	32	33	34	35	36	37	38	39	40
41	42							49	50

2 Trace the gray numbers.

2 points per question

51	52	53	54	55	56	57	58	59	60
61	62	63	64	65	66	67	68	69	70
71	72	73	74	75	76	77	78	79	80
81	82	83	84	85	86	87	88	89	90
91	92	93	94	95	96	97	98	99	100

16 © Kumon Publishing Co., Ltd.

3 Fill in the missing numbers.

3 points per question

51									60
61	62	63	64	65	66	67	68	69	70
71	72	73	74	75	76	77	78	79	80
81	82	83	84	85	86	87	88	89	90
91	92	93	94	95	96	97	98	99	100

4 Trace the gray numbers.

2 points per question

51	52	53	54	55	56	57	58	59	60
61	62	63	64	65	66	67	68	69	70
71	72	73	74	75	76	77	78	79	80
81	82	83	84	85	86	87	88	89	90
91	92	93	94	95	96	97	98	99	100

You're doing great! Let's keep counting!

Table of Numbers ◆To 100

Level ★★ Score /100

Date / /

Name

1 **Fill in the missing numbers.**

3 points per question

51	52	53	54	55	56	57	58	59	60
61									70
71	72	73	74	75	76	77	78	79	80
81	82	83	84	85	86	87	88	89	90
91	92	93	94	95	96	97	98	99	100

2 **Trace the gray numbers.**

2 points per question

51	52	53	54	55	56	57	58	59	60
61	62	63	64	65	66	67	68	69	70
71	72	73	74	75	76	77	78	79	80
81	82	83	84	85	86	87	88	89	90
91	92	93	94	95	96	97	98	99	100

3 Fill in the missing numbers.

3 points per question

51	52	53	54	55	56	57	58	59	60
61	62	63	64	65	66	67	68	69	70
71									80
81	82	83	84	85	86	87	88	89	90
91	92	93	94	95	96	97	98	99	100

4 Trace the gray numbers.

2 points per question

51	52	53	54	55	56	57	58	59	60
61	62	63	64	65	66	67	68	69	70
71	72	73	74	75	76	77	78	79	80
81	82	83	84	85	86	87	88	89	90
91	92	93	94	95	96	97	98	99	100

These are really big numbers, aren't they?

Table of Numbers ◆1 to 100

Level ★★

Score /100

Date / /

Name

1 **Fill in the missing numbers.** 2 points per question

51	52	53	54	55	56	57	58	59	60
61	62	63	64	65	66	67	68	69	70
71	72	73	74	75	76	77	78	79	80
81									90
91	92	93	94	95	96	97	98	99	100

2 **Trace the gray numbers.** 2 points per question

51	52	53	54	55	56	57	58	59	60
61	62	63	64	65	66	67	68	69	70
71	72	73	74	75	76	77	78	79	80
81	82	83	84	85	86	87	88	89	90
91	92	93	94	95	96	97	98	99	100

③ Fill in the missing numbers.

2 points per question

51	52	53	54	55	56	57	58	59	60
61	62	63	64	65	66	67	68	69	70
71	72	73	74	75	76	77	78	79	80
81	82	83	84	85	86	87	88	89	90
91									100

④ Fill in the missing numbers.

2 points per question

1									
11	12	13	14	15	16	17	18	19	20
21	22	23	24	25	26	27	28	29	30
41	42	43	44	45	46	47	48	49	50

Wow! You made it all the way to 100!

21

Table of Numbers ◆ 1 to 100

Level ★★

Date   /   /

Name

Score

/100

1 Fill in the missing numbers.

2 points per question

51	52	53	54	55	56	57	58	59	60
61	62	63	64	65	66	67	68	69	70
81	82	83	84	85	86	87	88	89	90

2 Fill in the missing numbers.

2 points per question

	2	3	4	5		7	8	9	10
	12	13	14	15		17	18	19	20
	22	23	24	25		27	28	29	30
	32	33	34	35		37	38	39	40
	42	43	44	45		47	48	49	50

③ Fill in the missing numbers.

2 points per question

1	2		4	5	6	7		9	10
11	12		14	15	16	17		19	20
21	22		24	25	26	27		29	30
31	32		34	35	36	37		39	40
41	42		44	45	46	47		49	50

④ Fill in the missing numbers.

2 points per question

51	52	53		55	56	57	58		60
61	62	63		65	66	67	68		70
71	72	73		75	76	77	78		80
81	82	83		85	86	87	88		90
91	92	93		95	96	97	98		100

Well done! Let's see what's next!

1 Fill in the missing numbers.

2 points per question

1	2	3	4	5					
					16	17	18	19	20
21	22	23	24	25	26	27	28	29	30
31	32	33	34	35	36	37	38	39	40
41	42	43	44	45	46	47	48	49	50

2 Fill in the missing numbers.

3 points per question

51	52	53							
			64	65	66	67	68	69	70
71	72	73	74	75	76	77	78	79	80
81	82	83	84	85	86	87	88	89	90
91	92	93	94	95	96	97	98	99	100

3 Fill in the missing numbers.

2 points per question

1	2	3	4	5	6	7	8	9	10
11	12	13	14	15					
					26	27	28	29	30
31	32	33	34	35	36	37	38	39	40
41	42	43	44	45	46	47	48	49	50

4 Fill in the missing numbers.

3 points per question

51	52	53	54	55	56	57	58	59	60
61	62	63							
			74	75	76	77	78	79	80
81	82	83	84	85	86	87	88	89	90
91	92	93	94	95	96	97	98	99	100

Did you fill in all of the missing numbers?

25

Table of Numbers ◆1 to 100

Level ★★

Date   /   /

Name

Score   /100

1 Fill in the missing numbers.

2 points per question

1	2	3	4	5	6	7	8	9	10
11	12	13	14	15	16	17	18	19	20
21	22	23	24						
				35	36	37	38	39	40
41	42	43	44	45	46	47	48	49	50

2 Fill in the missing numbers.

3 points per question

51	52	53	54	55	56	57	58	59	60
61	62	63	64	65	66	67	68	69	70
71	72								
		83	84	85	86	87	88	89	90
91	92	93	94	95	96	97	98	99	100

3 Fill in the missing numbers.

2 points per question

1	2	3	4	5	6	7	8	9	10
		13	14	15	16	17	18	19	20
21	22	23	24				28	29	30
31	32			35	36	37	38	39	40
41	42	43	44	45	46	47			

4 Fill in the missing numbers.

3 points per question

51	52			55	56	57	58	59	60
61	62	63	64			67	68	69	70
71	72	73	74	75	76			79	80
81	82	83	84	85	86	87	88		
		93	94	95	96	97	98	99	100

Are you ready to try even higher numbers?
Let's try!

Level ★ ★ ★

Date / /

Name

Score /100

1 Fill in the missing numbers.

2 points per question

61	62		64	65	66	67		69	
71		73	74	75	76	77	78		80
81	82	83		85		87	88	89	90
91	92	93	94		96		98		100
101	102	103	104	105	106	107	108	109	110

2 Fill in the missing numbers.

3 points per question

71	72	73	74	75		77	78		80
81		83		85	86		88	89	90
	92	93	94		96	97	98	99	100
101	102		104	105	106	107		109	
111	112	113	114	115	116	117	118	119	120

Fill in the missing numbers.

2 points per question

61		63	64	65	66	67	68		70
71	72	73	74	75	76		78	79	
81	82	83	84		86	87		89	90
91	92		94	95		97	98	99	100
	102	103		105	106	107	108	109	110

④

Fill in the missing numbers.

3 points per question

71	72		74	75	76	77		79	80
81	82	83	84	85		87	88		90
91	92	93		95	96		98	99	100
101		103	104		106	107	108	109	110
	112	113	114	115	116	117	118	119	

120? That's HUGE!

15
Adding 1 ◆1+1 to 10+1

Level
★★

Date
/ /

Name

Score

/100

1 **Write the number that comes next.**   2 points per question

(1) 1 ⟶ [2]   (6) 4 ⟶ [ ]

(2) 2 ⟶ [ ]   (7) 5 ⟶ [ ]

(3) 3 ⟶ [ ]   (8) 7 ⟶ [ ]

(4) 4 ⟶ [ ]   (9) 9 ⟶ [ ]

(5) 6 ⟶ [ ]   (10) 8 ⟶ [ ]

2 **Write the number that comes next.**   3 points per question

(1) 2 ⟶ [3]   (3) 5 ⟶ [ ]

$2 + 1 =$ [3] $5 + 1 =$ [ ]

(2) 3 ⟶ [ ]   (4) 6 ⟶ [ ]

$3 + 1 =$ [ ] $6 + 1 =$ [ ]

3 Read each number sentence as you trace it.

2 points per question

(1) $1 + 1 = 2$
One plus one equals two.

(2) $2 + 1 = 3$
Two plus one equals three.

(3) $3 + 1 = 4$
Three plus one equals four.

(4) $4 + 1 = 5$
Four plus one equals five.

(5) $5 + 1 = 6$
Five plus one equals six.

(6) $6 + 1 = 7$
Six plus one equals seven.

(7) $7 + 1 = 8$
Seven plus one equals eight.

(8) $8 + 1 = 9$
Eight plus one equals nine.

(9) $9 + 1 = 10$
Nine plus one equals ten.

(10) $10 + 1 = 11$
Ten plus one equals eleven.

6 + 1 is 7.
7 is one more than 6.

4 Add.

4 points per question

(1) $4 + 1 =$

(2) $5 + 1 =$

(3) $6 + 1 =$

(4) $1 + 1 =$

(5) $2 + 1 =$

(6) $3 + 1 =$

(7) $4 + 1 =$

(8) $6 + 1 =$

(9) $7 + 1 =$

(10) $8 + 1 =$

(11) $9 + 1 =$

(12) $10 + 1 =$

It's time to start practicing our addition.
Are you ready?

1 Add.

2 points per question

(1) $4 + 1 =$

(2) $3 + 1 =$

(3) $2 + 1 =$

(4) $1 + 1 =$

(5) $10 + 1 =$

(6) $9 + 1 =$

(7) $8 + 1 =$

(8) $7 + 1 =$

(9) $6 + 1 =$

(10) $5 + 1 =$

2 Add.

2 points per question

(1) $1 + 1 =$

(2) $3 + 1 =$

(3) $5 + 1 =$

(4) $7 + 1 =$

(5) $2 + 1 =$

(6) $4 + 1 =$

(7) $6 + 1 =$

(8) $8 + 1 =$

(9) $10 + 1 =$

(10) $9 + 1 =$

3 Add.

3 points per question

(1) 4 + 1 =

(2) 7 + 1 =

(3) 9 + 1 =

(4) 3 + 1 =

(5) 2 + 1 =

(6) 5 + 1 =

(7) 10 + 1 =

(8) 1 + 1 =

(9) 8 + 1 =

(10) 9 + 1 =

(11) 2 + 1 =

(12) 6 + 1 =

(13) 7 + 1 =

(14) 4 + 1 =

(15) 10 + 1 =

(16) 8 + 1 =

(17) 1 + 1 =

(18) 5 + 1 =

(19) 3 + 1 =

(20) 6 + 1 =

Good job! Now let's check your answers with your parents !

Date / /

Name

Score /100

1 Add.

2 points per question

(1) $6 + 1 =$

(2) $7 + 1 =$

(3) $8 + 1 =$

(4) $9 + 1 =$

(5) $10 + 1 =$

(6) $11 + 1 = 12$

(7) $12 + 1 = 13$

(8) $13 + 1 = 14$

(9) $14 + 1 =$

(10) $15 + 1 =$

2 Add.

3 points per question

(1) $7 + 1 =$

(2) $10 + 1 =$

(3) $13 + 1 =$

(4) $5 + 1 =$

(5) $15 + 1 =$

(6) $11 + 1 =$

(7) $9 + 1 =$

(8) $8 + 1 =$

(9) $12 + 1 =$

(10) $14 + 1 =$

3 Add.

2 points per question

(1) $11+1=$

(2) $12+1=$

(3) $13+1=$

(4) $14+1=$

(5) $15+1=$

(6) $16+1=17$

(7) $17+1=18$

(8) $18+1=19$

(9) $19+1=$

(10) $20+1=$

4 Add.

3 points per question

(1) $18+1=$

(2) $16+1=$

(3) $20+1=$

(4) $17+1=$

(5) $12+1=$

(6) $11+1=$

(7) $13+1=$

(8) $19+1=$

(9) $14+1=$

(10) $15+1=$

You're doing really well, keep it up!

1 Add.

2 points per question

(1) $16+1=$

(2) $17+1=$

(3) $18+1=$

(4) $19+1=$

(5) $20+1=$

(6) $21+1=22$

(7) $22+1=23$

(8) $23+1=24$

(9) $24+1=$

(10) $25+1=$

2 Add.

3 points per question

(1) $17+1=$

(2) $15+1=$

(3) $20+1=$

(4) $24+1=$

(5) $19+1=$

(6) $22+1=$

(7) $18+1=$

(8) $23+1=$

(9) $25+1=$

(10) $21+1=$

3 **Add.**

2 points per question

(1) $21+1=$

(2) $22+1=$

(3) $23+1=$

(4) $24+1=$

(5) $25+1=$

(6) $26+1=27$

(7) $27+1=28$

(8) $28+1=$

(9) $29+1=$

(10) $30+1=$

4 **Add.**

3 points per question

(1) $28+1=$

(2) $25+1=$

(3) $23+1=$

(4) $27+1=$

(5) $21+1=$

(6) $24+1=$

(7) $29+1=$

(8) $22+1=$

(9) $30+1=$

(10) $26+1=$

How many did you get right? Good job!

1 **Add.**

2 points per question

(1) 26+1 =

(2) 27+1 =

(3) 28+1 =

(4) 29+1 =

(5) 30+1 =

(6) 31+1 = 32

(7) 32+1 =

(8) 33+1 =

(9) 34+1 =

(10) 35+1 =

2 **Add.**

3 points per question

(1) 28+1 =

(2) 25+1 =

(3) 33+1 =

(4) 30+1 =

(5) 29+1 =

(6) 34+1 =

(7) 31+1 =

(8) 26+1 =

(9) 35+1 =

(10) 32+1 =

3 Add.

2 points per question

(1) $31 + 1 =$

(2) $32 + 1 =$

(3) $33 + 1 =$

(4) $34 + 1 =$

(5) $35 + 1 =$

(6) $36 + 1 =$

(7) $37 + 1 =$

(8) $38 + 1 =$

(9) $39 + 1 =$

(10) $40 + 1 =$

4 Add.

3 points per question

(1) $37 + 1 =$

(2) $36 + 1 =$

(3) $40 + 1 =$

(4) $38 + 1 =$

(5) $31 + 1 =$

(6) $39 + 1 =$

(7) $34 + 1 =$

(8) $33 + 1 =$

(9) $35 + 1 =$

(10) $32 + 1 =$

Have you mastered your +1 addition?

20 Adding 1 ◆ To 100＋1 and beyond

Date / / Name

1 Add.

2 points per question

(1) 41＋1 =

(2) 42＋1 =

(3) 43＋1 =

(4) 51＋1 =

(5) 52＋1 =

(6) 53＋1 =

(7) 44＋1 =

(8) 45＋1 =

(9) 46＋1 =

(10) 47＋1 =

(11) 54＋1 =

(12) 55＋1 =

(13) 56＋1 =

(14) 57＋1 =

(15) 48＋1 =

(16) 49＋1 =

(17) 50＋1 =

(18) 58＋1 =

(19) 59＋1 =

(20) 60＋1 =

© Kumon Publishing Co., Ltd.

2 Add.

3 points per question

(1) $66 + 1 =$

(2) $67 + 1 =$

(3) $68 + 1 =$

(4) $76 + 1 =$

(5) $77 + 1 =$

(6) $78 + 1 =$

(7) $86 + 1 =$

(8) $87 + 1 =$

(9) $88 + 1 =$

(10) $89 + 1 =$

(11) $96 + 1 =$

(12) $97 + 1 =$

(13) $98 + 1 =$

(14) $99 + 1 =$

(15) $101 + 1 =$

(16) $100 + 1 =$

(17) $108 + 1 =$

(18) $110 + 1 =$

(19) $109 + 1 =$

(20) $118 + 1 =$

Are you ready to move on to the next level?

Adding 2 ◆1+2 to 10+2

Level
 ★★

Date / /

Name

Score
/100

---

1 Trace the gray numbers and add.

2 points per question

(1)

| 1 | 2 | 3 → | 4 → | 5 | 6 | 7 |

$$3 + 2 = 5$$

(2)

| 4 | 5 | 6 → | 7 → | 8 | 9 | 10 |

$$6 + 2 = 8$$

(3)

| 3 | 4 | 5 → | 6 → | 7 | 8 | 9 |

$$5 + 2 =$$

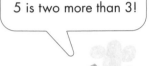

(1) 3 + 2 is 5.
5 is two more than 3!

---

2 Add.

3 points per question

| 1 | 2 | 3 | 4 | 5 | 6 | 7 | 8 | 9 | 10 |

(1) $1 + 2 =$

(2) $4 + 2 =$

(3) $6 + 2 =$

(4) $3 + 2 =$

(5) $5 + 2 =$

(6) $2 + 2 =$

(7) $7 + 2 =$

(8) $8 + 2 =$

3 **Read each number sentence as you trace it.** 3 points per question

(1) $1 + 2 = 3$
One   plus   two equals three.

(2) $2 + 2 = 4$
Two   plus   two equals four.

(3) $3 + 2 = 5$
Three   plus two equals five.

(4) $4 + 2 = 6$
Four   plus   two equals six.

(5) $5 + 2 = 7$
Five   plus   two equals seven.

(6) $6 + 2 = 8$
Six   plus   two equals eight.

(7) $7 + 2 = 9$
Seven   plus   two equals nine.

(8) $8 + 2 = 10$

(9) $9 + 2 = 11$

(10) $10 + 2 = 12$

4 **Add.** 4 points per question

(1) $4 + 2 =$

(2) $5 + 2 =$

(3) $6 + 2 =$

(4) $1 + 2 =$

(5) $2 + 2 =$

(6) $3 + 2 =$

(7) $7 + 2 =$

(8) $8 + 2 =$

(9) $9 + 2 =$

(10) $10 + 2 =$

When you're done, let's check your score!

43

22 Adding 2 ◆ 1+2 to 10+2

Level ★★

Score

/100

Date / /

Name

1 Add.

2 points per question

(1) 4 + 2 =

(2) 3 + 2 =

(3) 2 + 2 =

(4) 1 + 2 =

(5) 10 + 2 =

(6) 9 + 2 =

(7) 8 + 2 =

(8) 7 + 2 =

(9) 6 + 2 =

(10) 5 + 2 =

2 Add.

2 points per question

(1) 1 + 2 =

(2) 3 + 2 =

(3) 5 + 2 =

(4) 7 + 2 =

(5) 2 + 2 =

(6) 4 + 2 =

(7) 6 + 2 =

(8) 8 + 2 =

(9) 10 + 2 =

(10) 9 + 2 =

3 Add.

(1) $4 + 2 =$

(2) $7 + 2 =$

(3) $9 + 2 =$

(4) $3 + 2 =$

(5) $2 + 2 =$

(6) $5 + 2 =$

(7) $10 + 2 =$

(8) $1 + 2 =$

(9) $8 + 2 =$

(10) $9 + 2 =$

(11) $2 + 2 =$

(12) $6 + 2 =$

(13) $7 + 2 =$

(14) $4 + 2 =$

(15) $10 + 2 =$

(16) $8 + 2 =$

(17) $1 + 2 =$

(18) $5 + 2 =$

(19) $3 + 2 =$

(20) $6 + 2 =$

Keep up the great work!

23 Adding 2 ◆5+2 to 20+2

Level

Date   /   /

Name

Score
/100

1 Add.

2 points per question

(1) 6 + 2 =

(2) 7 + 2 =

(3) 8 + 2 =

(4) 9 + 2 =

(5) 10 + 2 =

(6) 11 + 2 =

(7) 12 + 2 =

(8) 13 + 2 =

(9) 14 + 2 =

(10) 15 + 2 =

2 Add.

3 points per question

(1) 5 + 2 =

(2) 6 + 2 =

(3) 10 + 2 =

(4) 12 + 2 =

(5) 8 + 2 =

(6) 11 + 2 =

(7) 13 + 2 =

(8) 15 + 2 =

(9) 9 + 2 =

(10) 14 + 2 =

3 Add.

2 points per question

(1) $11+2=$

(2) $12+2=$

(3) $13+2=$

(4) $14+2=$

(5) $15+2=$

(6) $16+2=$

(7) $17+2=$

(8) $18+2=$

(9) $19+2=$

(10) $20+2=$

4 Add.

3 points per question

(1) $14+2=$

(2) $16+2=$

(3) $15+2=$

(4) $11+2=$

(5) $17+2=$

(6) $12+2=$

(7) $20+2=$

(8) $19+2=$

(9) $13+2=$

(10) $18+2=$

When you're done, don't forget to check your answers!

24 Adding 2 ◆14+2 to 30+2 ★★★

Level ★★★

Date / /

Name

Score /100

---

1 **Add.**   2 points per question

(1) 16+2 =

(2) 17+2 =

(3) 18+2 =

(4) 19+2 =

(5) 20+2 =

(6) 21+2 =

(7) 22+2 =

(8) 23+2 =

(9) 24+2 =

(10) 25+2 =

---

2 **Add.**   3 points per question

(1) 14+2 =

(2) 20+2 =

(3) 23+2 =

(4) 21+2 =

(5) 16+2 =

(6) 22+2 =

(7) 25+2 =

(8) 18+2 =

(9) 24+2 =

(10) 19+2 =

---

3 **Add.**

2 points per question

(1) $21+2=$

(2) $22+2=$

(3) $23+2=$

(4) $24+2=$

(5) $25+2=$

(6) $26+2=$

(7) $27+2=$

(8) $28+2=$

(9) $29+2=$

(10) $30+2=$

4 **Add.**

3 points per question

(1) $27+2=$

(2) $25+2=$

(3) $24+2=$

(4) $26+2=$

(5) $28+2=$

(6) $30+2=$

(7) $22+2=$

(8) $20+2=$

(9) $23+2=$

(10) $29+2=$

Have you mastered your +2 addition?

25

Adding 2 ◆26+2 to 45+2 ★★★

Score /100

Date / /

Name

1 Add.

2 points per question

(1) $26+2=$

(2) $27+2=$

(3) $28+2=$

(4) $29+2=$

(5) $30+2=$

(6) $31+2=$

(7) $32+2=$

(8) $33+2=$

(9) $34+2=$

(10) $35+2=$

2 Add.

3 points per question

(1) $27+2=$

(2) $30+2=$

(3) $33+2=$

(4) $35+2=$

(5) $31+2=$

(6) $29+2=$

(7) $26+2=$

(8) $34+2=$

(9) $28+2=$

(10) $32+2=$

© Kumon Publishing Co., Ltd.

3 Add.

2 points per question

(1) $36+2=$

(2) $37+2=$

(3) $38+2=$

(4) $39+2=$

(5) $40+2=$

(6) $41+2=$

(7) $42+2=$

(8) $43+2=$

(9) $44+2=$

(10) $45+2=$

4 Add.

3 points per question

(1) $35+2=$

(2) $40+2=$

(3) $45+2=$

(4) $42+2=$

(5) $38+2=$

(6) $43+2=$

(7) $41+2=$

(8) $36+2=$

(9) $44+2=$

(10) $39+2=$

Are you ready for +3 addition? Let's go!

1 **Trace the gray numbers and add.**

2 points per question

(1)

| 1 | 2 → | 3 → | 4 → | 5 | 6 | 7 |

$$2 + 3 = 5$$

(1) 2 + 3 is 5.
5 is three more than 2.

(2)

| 2 | 3 | 4 → | 5 → | 6 → | 7 | 8 |

$$4 + 3 = 7$$

(3)

| 4 | 5 | 6 → | 7 → | 8 → | 9 | 10 |

$$6 + 3 =$$

2 **Add.**

3 points per question

| 1 | 2 | 3 | 4 | 5 | 6 | 7 | 8 | 9 | 10 |

(1) $1 + 3 =$

(2) $3 + 3 =$

(3) $2 + 3 =$

(4) $4 + 3 =$

(5) $5 + 3 =$

(6) $4 + 3 =$

(7) $6 + 3 =$

(8) $7 + 3 =$

3 **Read each number sentence as you trace it.** 3 points per question

(1) $1 + 3 = 4$
One   plus three equals four.

(2) $2 + 3 = 5$
Two   plus three equals five.

(3) $3 + 3 = 6$

(4) $4 + 3 = 7$

(5) $5 + 3 = 8$

(6) $6 + 3 = 9$

(7) $7 + 3 = 10$

(8) $8 + 3 = 11$

(9) $9 + 3 = 12$

(10) $10 + 3 = 13$

4 **Add.** 4 points per question

(1) $4 + 3 =$

(2) $5 + 3 =$

(3) $6 + 3 =$

(4) $1 + 3 =$

(5) $2 + 3 =$

(6) $3 + 3 =$

(7) $7 + 3 =$

(8) $8 + 3 =$

(9) $9 + 3 =$

(10) $10 + 3 =$

I knew you could do it!
Let's practice some more!

53

1 Add.

2 points per question

(1) $1 + 3 =$

(2) $3 + 3 =$

(3) $5 + 3 =$

(4) $7 + 3 =$

(5) $2 + 3 =$

(6) $4 + 3 =$

(7) $6 + 3 =$

(8) $8 + 3 =$

(9) $10 + 3 =$

(10) $9 + 3 =$

2 Add.

3 points per question

(1) $4 + 3 =$

(2) $7 + 3 =$

(3) $9 + 3 =$

(4) $10 + 3 =$

(5) $2 + 3 =$

(6) $5 + 3 =$

(7) $3 + 3 =$

(8) $1 + 3 =$

(9) $6 + 3 =$

(10) $8 + 3 =$

3 **Add.**

2 points per question

(1) $6 + 3 =$

(2) $7 + 3 =$

(3) $8 + 3 =$

(4) $9 + 3 =$

(5) $10 + 3 =$

(6) $11 + 3 =$

(7) $12 + 3 =$

(8) $13 + 3 =$

(9) $14 + 3 =$

(10) $15 + 3 =$

4 **Add.**

3 points per question

(1) $7 + 3 =$

(2) $10 + 3 =$

(3) $13 + 3 =$

(4) $11 + 3 =$

(5) $14 + 3 =$

(6) $12 + 3 =$

(7) $8 + 3 =$

(8) $5 + 3 =$

(9) $15 + 3 =$

(10) $9 + 3 =$

When you're done, let's check your score!

Adding 3 ◆11+3 to 25+3

Level ★★★

Date / /

Name

Score /100

---

1 Add.

2 points per question

(1) 11+3=

(2) 12+3=

(3) 13+3=

(4) 14+3=

(5) 15+3=

(6) 16+3=

(7) 17+3=

(8) 18+3=

(9) 19+3=

(10) 20+3=

---

2 Add.

3 points per question

(1) 14+3=

(2) 15+3=

(3) 16+3=

(4) 17+3=

(5) 8 +3=

(6) 9 +3=

(7) 10+3=

(8) 18+3=

(9) 19+3=

(10) 20+3=

---

3 **Add.**

2 points per question

(1) $7+3=$

(2) $17+3=$

(3) $18+3=$

(4) $19+3=$

(5) $20+3=$

(6) $21+3=$

(7) $22+3=$

(8) $23+3=$

(9) $24+3=$

(10) $25+3=$

4 **Add.**

3 points per question

(1) $14+3=$

(2) $24+3=$

(3) $11+3=$

(4) $21+3=$

(5) $23+3=$

(6) $25+3=$

(7) $17+3=$

(8) $18+3=$

(9) $22+3=$

(10) $19+3=$

Have you mastered your +3 addition?

1 Add.

2 points per question

(1) $1 + 1 =$

(2) $1 + 2 =$

(3) $1 + 3 =$

(4) $1 + 4 = 5$

(5) $4 + 1 =$

(6) $4 + 2 =$

(7) $4 + 3 =$

(8) $4 + 4 =$

(9) $2 + 2 =$

(10) $2 + 3 =$

(11) $2 + 4 =$

(12) $5 + 2 =$

(13) $5 + 3 =$

(14) $5 + 4 =$

(15) $3 + 2 =$

(16) $3 + 3 =$

(17) $3 + 4 =$

(18) $6 + 2 =$

(19) $6 + 3 =$

(20) $6 + 4 =$

2 **Trace the gray numbers while adding.** 3 points per question

(1) $1 + 4 = 5$

(2) $2 + 4 = 6$

(3) $3 + 4 = 7$

(4) $4 + 4 = 8$

(5) $5 + 4 = 9$

(6) $6 + 4 = 10$

(7) $7 + 4 = 11$

(8) $8 + 4 = 12$

(9) $9 + 4 = 13$

(10) $10 + 4 = 14$

3 **Add.** 3 points per question

(1) $1 + 4 =$

(2) $3 + 4 =$

(3) $5 + 4 =$

(4) $2 + 4 =$

(5) $4 + 4 =$

(6) $6 + 4 =$

(7) $8 + 4 =$

(8) $10 + 4 =$

(9) $9 + 4 =$

(10) $7 + 4 =$

It's +4 addition time!

59

Adding 4 ◆To 19+4

Date / /

Name

Score /100

1 Add.

2 points per question

(1) $7 + 4 =$

(2) $3 + 4 =$

(3) $8 + 4 =$

(4) $9 + 4 =$

(5) $10 + 4 =$

(6) $11 + 4 =$

(7) $12 + 4 =$

(8) $13 + 4 =$

(9) $14 + 4 =$

(10) $15 + 4 =$

2 Add.

3 points per question

(1) $9 + 4 =$

(2) $3 + 4 =$

(3) $13 + 4 =$

(4) $11 + 4 =$

(5) $12 + 4 =$

(6) $5 + 4 =$

(7) $15 + 4 =$

(8) $8 + 4 =$

(9) $6 + 4 =$

(10) $14 + 4 =$

3 Add.

2 points per question

(1) $13+4=$

(2) $14+4=$

(3) $15+4=$

(4) $16+4=$

(5) $17+4=$

(6) $18+4=$

(7) $19+4=$

(8) $9+4=$

(9) $8+4=$

(10) $7+4=$

4 Add.

3 points per question

(1) $8+4=$

(2) $18+4=$

(3) $14+4=$

(4) $7+4=$

(5) $17+4=$

(6) $5+4=$

(7) $13+4=$

(8) $9+4=$

(9) $16+4=$

(10) $18+4=$

Have you mastered your +4 addition?

Adding 5 ◆To 10 + 5

Date / /

Name

Level
★ ★

Score
/100

1 Add.

2 points per question

(1) $3 + 1 =$

(2) $3 + 2 =$

(3) $3 + 3 =$

(4) $4 + 1 =$

(5) $4 + 2 =$

(6) $4 + 3 =$

(7) $4 + 4 =$

(8) $4 + 5 = 9$

(9) $2 + 3 =$

(10) $2 + 4 =$

(11) $2 + 5 =$

(12) $5 + 1 =$

(13) $5 + 2 =$

(14) $5 + 3 =$

(15) $5 + 4 =$

(16) $5 + 5 =$

(17) $6 + 2 =$

(18) $6 + 3 =$

(19) $6 + 4 =$

(20) $6 + 5 =$

2 Trace the gray numbers while adding.

3 points per question

(1) $1 + 5 = 6$

(2) $2 + 5 = 7$

(3) $3 + 5 = 8$

(4) $4 + 5 = 9$

(5) $5 + 5 = 10$

(6) $6 + 5 = 11$

(7) $7 + 5 = 12$

(8) $8 + 5 = 13$

(9) $9 + 5 = 14$

(10) $10 + 5 = 15$

3 Add.

3 points per question

(1) $2 + 5 =$

(2) $4 + 5 =$

(3) $1 + 5 =$

(4) $3 + 5 =$

(5) $5 + 5 =$

(6) $7 + 5 =$

(7) $9 + 5 =$

(8) $6 + 5 =$

(9) $8 + 5 =$

(10) $10 + 5 =$

When you're done, don't forget to check your answers!

1 **Add.**

2 points per question

(1) $9 + 5 =$

(2) $10 + 5 =$

(3) $11 + 5 =$

(4) $2 + 5 =$

(5) $12 + 5 =$

(6) $3 + 5 =$

(7) $13 + 5 =$

(8) $4 + 5 =$

(9) $14 + 5 =$

(10) $7 + 5 =$

2 **Add.**

3 points per question

(1) $5 + 5 =$

(2) $8 + 5 =$

(3) $11 + 5 =$

(4) $6 + 5 =$

(5) $9 + 5 =$

(6) $12 + 5 =$

(7) $7 + 5 =$

(8) $10 + 5 =$

(9) $13 + 5 =$

(10) $14 + 5 =$

3 Add.

2 points per question

(1) $13+5=$

(2) $14+5=$

(3) $15+5=$

(4) $16+5=$

(5) $17+5=$

(6) $18+5=$

(7) $19+5=$

(8) $10+5=$

(9) $11+5=$

(10) $12+5=$

4 Add.

3 points per question

(1) $6+5=$

(2) $16+5=$

(3) $8+5=$

(4) $18+5=$

(5) $3+5=$

(6) $13+5=$

(7) $9+5=$

(8) $19+5=$

(9) $7+5=$

(10) $17+5=$

Have you mastered your +5 addition?

1 **Add.**

2 points per question

(1) $1 + 3 =$

(2) $1 + 4 =$

(3) $1 + 5 =$

(4) $1 + 6 = 7$

(5) $4 + 3 =$

(6) $4 + 4 =$

(7) $4 + 5 =$

(8) $4 + 6 =$

(9) $2 + 4 =$

(10) $2 + 5 =$

(11) $2 + 6 =$

(12) $5 + 4 =$

(13) $5 + 5 =$

(14) $5 + 6 =$

(15) $3 + 4 =$

(16) $3 + 5 =$

(17) $3 + 6 =$

(18) $6 + 4 =$

(19) $6 + 5 =$

(20) $6 + 6 =$

2 Add.

3 points per question

(1) $1 + 6 = 7$

(2) $2 + 6 = 8$

(3) $3 + 6 = 9$

(4) $4 + 6 =$

(5) $5 + 6 =$

(6) $6 + 6 =$

(7) $7 + 6 =$

(8) $8 + 6 =$

(9) $9 + 6 =$

(10) $10 + 6 =$

3 Add.

3 points per question

(1) $4 + 6 =$

(2) $5 + 6 =$

(3) $6 + 6 =$

(4) $1 + 6 =$

(5) $2 + 6 =$

(6) $3 + 6 =$

(7) $7 + 6 =$

(8) $8 + 6 =$

(9) $9 + 6 =$

(10) $10 + 6 =$

You've made a lot of progress, keep up the good work!

Date   /   /

Name

Score

/100

1 Add.   2 points per question

(1) 1 +6 =

(2) 3 +6 =

(3) 2 +6 =

(4) 4 +6 =

(5) 6 +6 =

(6) 5 +6 =

(7) 7 +6 =

(8) 9 +6 =

(9) 10+6 =

(10) 8 +6 =

2 Add.   2 points per question

(1) 10+6 =

(2) 11+6 =

(3) 12+6 =

(4) 13+6 =

(5) 14+6 =

(6) 15+6 =

(7) 3 +6 =

(8) 13+6 =

(9) 4 +6 =

(10) 14+6 =

3 **Add.**

3 points per question

(1) $7 + 6 =$

(2) $12 + 6 =$

(3) $14 + 6 =$

(4) $5 + 6 =$

(5) $2 + 6 =$

(6) $15 + 6 =$

(7) $9 + 6 =$

(8) $13 + 6 =$

(9) $8 + 6 =$

(10) $11 + 6 =$

(11) $1 + 6 =$

(12) $7 + 6 =$

(13) $13 + 6 =$

(14) $2 + 6 =$

(15) $8 + 6 =$

(16) $14 + 6 =$

(17) $3 + 6 =$

(18) $9 + 6 =$

(19) $15 + 6 =$

(20) $12 + 6 =$

Have you mastered your +6 addition?

1 Add.

2 points per question

(1) $1 + 5 =$

(2) $1 + 6 =$

(3) $1 + 7 = 8$

(4) $4 + 6 =$

(5) $4 + 7 =$

(6) $3 + 5 =$

(7) $3 + 6 =$

(8) $3 + 7 =$

(9) $6 + 6 =$

(10) $6 + 7 =$

2 Add.

3 points per question

(1) $1 + 7 = 8$

(2) $2 + 7 = 9$

(3) $3 + 7 =$

(4) $4 + 7 =$

(5) $5 + 7 =$

(6) $6 + 7 =$

(7) $7 + 7 =$

(8) $8 + 7 =$

(9) $9 + 7 =$

(10) $10 + 7 =$

3 **Add.**

2 points per question

(1) $4 + 7 =$

(2) $5 + 7 =$

(3) $6 + 7 =$

(4) $1 + 7 =$

(5) $2 + 7 =$

(6) $3 + 7 =$

(7) $7 + 7 =$

(8) $8 + 7 =$

(9) $9 + 7 =$

(10) $10 + 7 =$

4 **Add.**

3 points per question

(1) $2 + 7 =$

(2) $1 + 7 =$

(3) $3 + 7 =$

(4) $5 + 7 =$

(5) $4 + 7 =$

(6) $6 + 7 =$

(7) $8 + 7 =$

(8) $10 + 7 =$

(9) $9 + 7 =$

(10) $7 + 7 =$

How are you doing with your +7 addition?

Adding 7 & 8

Date   /   /

Name

Level
★ ★ ★

Score
/100

1 Add.

2 points per question

(1) $9 + 7 =$

(2) $10 + 7 =$

(3) $11 + 7 =$

(4) $12 + 7 =$

(5) $2 + 7 =$

(6) $3 + 7 =$

(7) $13 + 7 =$

(8) $14 + 7 =$

(9) $15 + 7 =$

(10) $5 + 7 =$

2 Add.

3 points per question

(1) $5 + 7 =$

(2) $11 + 7 =$

(3) $8 + 7 =$

(4) $13 + 7 =$

(5) $4 + 7 =$

(6) $15 + 7 =$

(7) $9 + 7 =$

(8) $14 + 7 =$

(9) $10 + 7 =$

(10) $3 + 7 =$

3 Add.

2 points per question

(1) $1 + 6 =$

(2) $1 + 7 =$

(3) $1 + 8 = 9$

(4) $4 + 7 =$

(5) $4 + 8 =$

(6) $3 + 7 =$

(7) $3 + 8 =$

(8) $6 + 6 =$

(9) $6 + 7 =$

(10) $6 + 8 =$

4 Add.

3 points per question

(1) $1 + 8 = 9$

(2) $2 + 8 =$

(3) $3 + 8 =$

(4) $4 + 8 =$

(5) $5 + 8 =$

(6) $6 + 8 =$

(7) $7 + 8 =$

(8) $8 + 8 =$

(9) $9 + 8 =$

(10) $10 + 8 =$

Nice work! Let's check your score!

1 **Add.**

2 points per question

(1) 4 + 8 =

(2) 5 + 8 =

(3) 6 + 8 =

(4) 1 + 8 =

(5) 2 + 8 =

(6) 3 + 8 =

(7) 7 + 8 =

(8) 8 + 8 =

(9) 9 + 8 =

(10) 10 + 8 =

2 **Add.**

3 points per question

(1) 8 + 8 =

(2) 5 + 8 =

(3) 10 + 8 =

(4) 7 + 8 =

(5) 1 + 8 =

(6) 6 + 8 =

(7) 3 + 8 =

(8) 2 + 8 =

(9) 9 + 8 =

(10) 4 + 8 =

3 **Add.**

2 points per question

(1) $9 + 8 =$

(2) $10 + 8 =$

(3) $11 + 8 =$

(4) $12 + 8 =$

(5) $2 + 8 =$

(6) $3 + 8 =$

(7) $13 + 8 =$

(8) $14 + 8 =$

(9) $15 + 8 =$

(10) $7 + 8 =$

4 **Add.**

3 points per question

(1) $7 + 8 =$

(2) $13 + 8 =$

(3) $5 + 8 =$

(4) $14 + 8 =$

(5) $9 + 8 =$

(6) $3 + 8 =$

(7) $1 + 8 =$

(8) $11 + 8 =$

(9) $4 + 8 =$

(10) $15 + 8 =$

Have you mastered your +8 addition?

Level ★★★

Date   /   /

Name

Score   /100

1 **Add.**

2 points per question

(1) $1 + 7 =$

(2) $1 + 8 =$

(3) $1 + 9 = 10$

(4) $4 + 8 =$

(5) $4 + 9 =$

(6) $2 + 7 =$

(7) $2 + 8 =$

(8) $2 + 9 =$

(9) $5 + 8 =$

(10) $5 + 9 =$

2 **Add.**

3 points per question

(1) $1 + 9 =$

(2) $2 + 9 =$

(3) $3 + 9 =$

(4) $4 + 9 =$

(5) $5 + 9 =$

(6) $6 + 9 =$

(7) $7 + 9 =$

(8) $8 + 9 =$

(9) $9 + 9 =$

(10) $10 + 9 =$

3 **Add.**

2 points per question

(1) $3 + 9 =$

(2) $8 + 9 =$

(3) $5 + 9 =$

(4) $1 + 9 =$

(5) $7 + 9 =$

(6) $4 + 9 =$

(7) $9 + 9 =$

(8) $2 + 9 =$

(9) $10 + 9 =$

(10) $6 + 9 =$

4 **Add.**

3 points per question

(1) $8 + 9 =$

(2) $9 + 9 =$

(3) $10 + 9 =$

(4) $11 + 9 =$

(5) $12 + 9 =$

(6) $13 + 9 =$

(7) $6 + 9 =$

(8) $8 + 9 =$

(9) $3 + 9 =$

(10) $13 + 9 =$

How are you doing with your + 9 addition?

77

Date   /   /

Name

Level ★ ★ ★

Score
/100

1 Add.

2 points per question

(1) 7 + 9 =

(2) 6 + 9 =

(3) 9 + 9 =

(4) 8 + 9 =

(5) 10+ 9 =

(6) 11+ 9 =

(7) 13+ 9 =

(8) 14+ 9 =

(9) 15+ 9 =

(10) 12+ 9 =

2 Add.

3 points per question

(1) 1 +10= 11

(2) 2 +10=

(3) 3 +10=

(4) 4 +10=

(5) 5 +10=

(6) 6 +10=

(7) 7 +10=

(8) 8 +10=

(9) 9 +10=

(10) 10+10=

3 Add.

2 points per question

(1) $9 + 9 =$

(2) $5 + 9 =$

(3) $10 + 9 =$

(4) $7 + 9 =$

(5) $12 + 9 =$

(6) $14 + 9 =$

(7) $5 + 9 =$

(8) $15 + 9 =$

(9) $8 + 9 =$

(10) $11 + 9 =$

4 Add.

3 points per question

(1) $7 + 10 =$

(2) $6 + 10 =$

(3) $9 + 10 =$

(4) $8 + 10 =$

(5) $10 + 10 =$

(6) $11 + 10 =$

(7) $13 + 10 =$

(8) $14 + 10 =$

(9) $12 + 10 =$

(10) $15 + 10 =$

Have you mastered your +10 addition?

Adding ◆Sums up to 16

Level ★★★

Date / /

Name

Score
/100

1 Add.

2 points per question

(1) 8 + 1 =

(2) 12 + 2 =

(3) 9 + 2 =

(4) 13 + 3 =

(5) 8 + 3 =

(6) 11 + 4 =

(7) 9 + 4 =

(8) 10 + 5 =

(9) 8 + 5 =

(10) 10 + 6 =

(11) 8 + 6 =

(12) 4 + 7 =

(13) 6 + 7 =

(14) 3 + 8 =

(15) 6 + 8 =

(16) 6 + 9 =

(17) 4 + 9 =

(18) 2 + 10 =

(19) 6 + 10 =

(20) 5 + 9 =

(21) 3 + 9 =

(22) 8 + 8 =

(23) 6 + 8 =

(24) 9 + 7 =

(25) 7 + 9 =

Remember that the order doesn't matter.
For example,
(24) 9 + 7 equals (25) 7 + 9.

2 Add.

(1) $9 + 5 =$

(2) $9 + 6 =$

(3) $10 + 5 =$

(4) $11 + 4 =$

(5) $11 + 5 =$

(6) $12 + 4 =$

(7) $12 + 3 =$

(8) $13 + 2 =$

(9) $13 + 3 =$

(10) $14 + 2 =$

(11) $14 + 1 =$

(12) $14 + 0 = 14$

(13) $12 + 2 =$

(14) $11 + 3 =$

(15) $10 + 6 =$

(16) $6 + 10 =$

(17) $5 + 11 =$

(18) $2 + 11 =$

(19) $1 + 12 =$

(20) $4 + 12 =$

(21) $1 + 13 =$

(22) $2 + 13 =$

(23) $1 + 14 =$

(24) $2 + 14 =$

(25) $1 + 15 =$

Any number plus zero is the same number.

Good job! Don't forget to check your answers.

81

Adding ◆Sums up to 20

Level ★★★

Date   /   /

Name

Score

/100

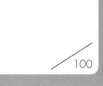

1 **Add.**

2 points per question

(1) $7 + 7 =$

(2) $8 + 7 =$

(3) $9 + 7 =$

(4) $10 + 3 =$

(5) $10 + 8 =$

(6) $11 + 4 =$

(7) $11 + 7 =$

(8) $12 + 6 =$

(9) $12 + 3 =$

(10) $13 + 4 =$

(11) $13 + 5 =$

(12) $14 + 4 =$

(13) $14 + 2 =$

(14) $15 + 3 =$

(15) $16 + 2 =$

(16) $17 + 1 =$

(17) $2 + 10 =$

(18) $4 + 11 =$

(19) $7 + 11 =$

(20) $5 + 12 =$

(21) $4 + 13 =$

(22) $3 + 14 =$

(23) $2 + 16 =$

(24) $2 + 15 =$

(25) $1 + 17 =$

2 Add.

(1) $10 + 9 =$

(2) $11 + 7 =$

(3) $11 + 9 =$

(4) $12 + 8 =$

(5) $12 + 6 =$

(6) $13 + 7 =$

(7) $14 + 5 =$

(8) $15 + 3 =$

(9) $16 + 4 =$

(10) $17 + 2 =$

(11) $18 + 1 =$

(12) $19 + 0 =$

(13) $6 + 11 =$

(14) $8 + 11 =$

(15) $7 + 12 =$

(16) $8 + 12 =$

(17) $5 + 13 =$

(18) $7 + 13 =$

(19) $5 + 14 =$

(20) $3 + 15 =$

(21) $5 + 15 =$

(22) $3 + 16 =$

(23) $3 + 17 =$

(24) $2 + 18 =$

(25) $1 + 19 =$

Wow! You've learned a lot so far!

Adding ◆Sums up to 28

Date / /

Name

Score

/100

1 **Add.**

2 points per question

(1) $5 + 8 =$

(2) $7 + 9 =$

(3) $6 + 9 =$

(4) $8 + 6 =$

(5) $7 + 10 =$

(6) $9 + 10 =$

(7) $7 + 11 =$

(8) $8 + 11 =$

(9) $4 + 12 =$

(10) $7 + 12 =$

(11) $9 + 12 =$

(12) $7 + 13 =$

(13) $9 + 13 =$

(14) $4 + 14 =$

(15) $8 + 14 =$

(16) $5 + 15 =$

(17) $9 + 15 =$

(18) $8 + 16 =$

(19) $3 + 16 =$

(20) $4 + 17 =$

(21) $5 + 17 =$

(22) $6 + 18 =$

(23) $5 + 18 =$

(24) $3 + 19 =$

(25) $5 + 19 =$

© Kumon Publishing Co., Ltd.

2 Add.

(1) $8 + 8 =$

(2) $13 + 6 =$

(3) $13 + 10 =$

(4) $12 + 10 =$

(5) $13 + 11 =$

(6) $15 + 11 =$

(7) $14 + 12 =$

(8) $15 + 12 =$

(9) $16 + 12 =$

(10) $13 + 13 =$

(11) $15 + 13 =$

(12) $12 + 13 =$

(13) $9 + 14 =$

(14) $12 + 14 =$

(15) $8 + 15 =$

(16) $11 + 15 =$

(17) $10 + 16 =$

(18) $11 + 16 =$

(19) $8 + 17 =$

(20) $9 + 17 =$

(21) $10 + 18 =$

(22) $8 + 18 =$

(23) $5 + 18 =$

(24) $7 + 19 =$

(25) $9 + 19 =$

Are you ready to review what you've learned?

43 Review

Date   /   /

Name

Level ★★★

Score

/100

1 Fill in the missing numbers.

2 points per question

61	62	63		65	66	67	68	69	70
71	72	73	74	75	76		78	79	
81		83	84	85	86	87	88	89	90
	92	93	94	95	96	97	98		100

2 Add.

2 points per question

(1) 6 + 1 =

(2) 9 + 1 =

(3) 7 + 1 =

(4) 8 + 2 =

(5) 5 + 2 =

(6) 4 + 2 =

(7) 7 + 3 =

(8) 6 + 3 =

(9) 9 + 4 =

(10) 8 + 4 =

(11) 6 + 4 =

(12) 7 + 4 =

(13) 7 + 5 =

(14) 9 + 5 =

(15) 8 + 5 =

(16) 5 + 5 =

86   © Kumon Publishing Co., Ltd.

3 Add.

2 points per question

(1) $3 + 6 =$

(2) $5 + 6 =$

(3) $7 + 6 =$

(4) $4 + 7 =$

(5) $6 + 7 =$

(6) $8 + 7 =$

(7) $2 + 8 =$

(8) $6 + 8 =$

(9) $9 + 8 =$

(10) $7 + 9 =$

(11) $5 + 9 =$

(12) $8 + 9 =$

4 Add.

2 points per question

(1) $6 + 4 =$

(2) $9 + 3 =$

(3) $7 + 5 =$

(4) $8 + 6 =$

(5) $5 + 7 =$

(6) $3 + 8 =$

(7) $6 + 9 =$

(8) $4 + 8 =$

(9) $4 + 7 =$

(10) $2 + 5 =$

(11) $9 + 6 =$

(12) $8 + 4 =$

(13) $6 + 1 =$

(14) $9 + 9 =$

(15) $8 + 5 =$

(16) $3 + 0 =$

Congratulations! You are ready for **Grade 1 Subtraction**!

(1)(2) Writing Numbers ◆1 to 6, 5 to 10   pp 2-5

Advice

Keep practicing your numbers, and remember the numbers 1 through 10.

(3) Writing Numbers ◆1 to 10   pp 6, 7

(1)

1	2	3	4	5
1	2	3	4	5

6	7	8	9	10
6	7	8	9	10

(2)

1	2	3	4	5

6	7	8	9	10

(3)

1	2	3	4	5
6	7	8	9	10

(4)

3	4	1	2	0

8	7	6	10	9

(4) Writing Numbers ◆1 to 15   pp 8, 9

(1)

1	2	3	4	5
6	7	8	9	10

(2)

3	6	4	1	9

5	8	2	7	0

(3)

1	2	3	4	5
6	7	8	9	10
11	12	13	14	15

(4)

1	2	3	4	5
6	7	8	9	10
11	12	13	14	15

1	2	3	4	5
6	7	8	9	10
11	12	13	14	15

(5) Writing Numbers ◆1 to 20   pp 10, 11

(1)

1	2	3	4	5
6	7	8	9	10
11	12	13	14	15
16	17	18	19	20

(2)

1	2	3	4	5
6	7	8	9	10
11	12	13	14	15

(3)

11	12	13	14	15
16	17	18	19	20

(4)

1	2	3	4	5
6	7	8	9	10
11	12	13	14	15
16	17	18	19	20

(5)

11	12	13	14	15
16	17	18	19	20

(6)

16	17	18	19	20

17	16	19	18	20

(6) Table of Numbers ◆1 to 30   pp 12, 13

(1)

1	2	3	4	5	6	7	8	9	10
11	12	13	14	15	16	17	18	19	20
21	22	23	24	25	26	27	28	29	30

(2)

1	2	3	4	5	6	7	8	9	10
11	12	13	14	15	16	17	18	19	20
21	22	23	24	25	26	27	28	29	30

(3)

1	2	3	4	5	6	7	8	9	10
11	12	13	14	15	16	17	18	19	20
21	22	23	24	25	26	27	28	29	30

(4)

1	2	3	4	5	6	7	8	9	10
11	12	13	14	15	16	17	18	19	20
21	22	23	24	25	26	27	28	29	30

(7) Table of Numbers ◆1 to 50   pp 14, 15

(1)

1	2	3	4	5	6	7	8	9	10
11	12	13	14	15	16	17	18	19	20
21	22	23	24	25	26	27	28	29	30

(2)

1	2	3	4	5	6	7	8	9	10
11	12	13	14	15	16	17	18	19	20
21	22	23	24	25	26	27	28	29	30
31	32	33	34	35	36	37	38	39	40

(3)

1	2	3	4	5	6	7	8	9	10
11	12	13	14	15	16	17	18	19	20
21	22	23	24	25	26	27	28	29	30
31	32	33	34	35	36	37	38	39	40

(4)

1	2	3	4	5	6	7	8	9	10
11	12	13	14	15	16	17	18	19	20
21	22	23	24	25	26	27	28	29	30
31	32	33	34	35	36	37	38	39	40
41	42	43	44	45	46	47	48	49	50

(8) Table of Numbers ◆1 to 100

pp 16, 17

(1)

1	2	3	4	5	6	7	8	9	10
11	12	13	14	15	16	17	18	19	20
21	22	23	24	25	26	27	28	29	30
31	32	33	34	35	36	37	38	39	40
41	42	43	44	45	46	47	48	49	50

(2)

51	52	53	54	55	56	57	58	59	60
61	62	63	64	65	66	67	68	69	70
71	72	73	74	75	76	77	78	79	80
81	82	83	84	85	86	87	88	89	90
91	92	93	94	95	96	97	98	99	100

(3)

51	52	53	54	55	56	57	58	59	60
61	62	63	64	65	66	67	68	69	70
71	72	73	74	75	76	77	78	79	80
81	82	83	84	85	86	87	88	89	90
91	92	93	94	95	96	97	98	99	100

(4)

51	52	53	54	55	56	57	58	59	60
61	62	63	64	65	66	67	68	69	70
71	72	73	74	75	76	77	78	79	80
81	82	83	84	85	86	87	88	89	90
91	92	93	94	95	96	97	98	99	100

(9) Table of Numbers ◆To 100

pp 18, 19

(1)

51	52	53	54	55	56	57	58	59	60
61	62	63	64	65	66	67	68	69	70
71	72	73	74	75	76	77	78	79	80
81	82	83	84	85	86	87	88	89	90
91	92	93	94	95	96	97	98	99	100

(2)

51	52	53	54	55	56	57	58	59	60
61	62	63	64	65	66	67	68	69	70
71	72	73	74	75	76	77	78	79	80
81	82	83	84	85	86	87	88	89	90
91	92	93	94	95	96	97	98	99	100

(3)

51	52	53	54	55	56	57	58	59	60
61	62	63	64	65	66	67	68	69	70
71	72	73	74	75	76	77	78	79	80
81	82	83	84	85	86	87	88	89	90
91	92	93	94	95	96	97	98	99	100

(4)

51	52	53	54	55	56	57	58	59	60
61	62	63	64	65	66	67	68	69	70
71	72	73	74	75	76	77	78	79	80
81	82	83	84	85	86	87	88	89	90
91	92	93	94	95	96	97	98	99	100

(10) Table of Numbers ◆1 to 100

pp 20, 21

(1)

51	52	53	54	55	56	57	58	59	60
61	62	63	64	65	66	67	68	69	70
71	72	73	74	75	76	77	78	79	80
81	82	83	84	85	86	87	88	89	90
91	92	93	94	95	96	97	98	99	100

(2)

51	52	53	54	55	56	57	58	59	60
61	62	63	64	65	66	67	68	69	70
71	72	73	74	75	76	77	78	79	80
81	82	83	84	85	86	87	88	89	90
91	92	93	94	95	96	97	98	99	100

3

51	52	53	54	55	56	57	58	59	60
61	62	63	64	65	66	67	68	69	70
71	72	73	74	75	76	77	78	79	80
81	82	83	84	85	86	87	88	89	90
91	92	93	94	95	96	97	98	99	100

4

1	2	3	4	5	6	7	8	9	10
11	12	13	14	15	16	17	18	19	20
21	22	23	24	25	26	27	28	29	30
31	32	33	34	35	36	37	38	39	40
41	42	43	44	45	46	47	48	49	50

11 Table of Numbers ♦1 to 100

1

51	52	53	54	55	56	57	58	59	60
61	62	63	64	65	66	67	68	69	70
71	72	73	74	75	76	77	78	79	80
81	82	83	84	85	86	87	88	89	90
91	92	93	94	95	96	97	98	99	100

2

1	2	3	4	5	6	7	8	9	10
11	12	13	14	15	16	17	18	19	20
21	22	23	24	25	26	27	28	29	30
31	32	33	34	35	36	37	38	39	40
41	42	43	44	45	46	47	48	49	50

3

1	2	3	4	5	6	7	8	9	10
11	12	13	14	15	16	17	18	19	20
21	22	23	24	25	26	27	28	29	30
31	32	33	34	35	36	37	38	39	40
41	42	43	44	45	46	47	48	49	50

4

51	52	53	54	55	56	57	58	59	60
61	62	63	64	65	66	67	68	69	70
71	72	73	74	75	76	77	78	79	80
81	82	83	84	85	86	87	88	89	90
91	92	93	94	95	96	97	98	99	100

Advice

In a vertical line on the number board, all of the numbers in the ones place are the same! You can also see that the numbers in the tens place all increase by one as you go down the line.

12 Table of Numbers ♦1 to 100

1

1	2	3	4	5	6	7	8	9	10
11	12	13	14	15	16	17	18	19	20
21	22	23	24	25	26	27	28	29	30
31	32	33	34	35	36	37	38	39	40
41	42	43	44	45	46	47	48	49	50

2

51	52	53	54	55	56	57	58	59	60
61	62	63	64	65	66	67	68	69	70
71	72	73	74	75	76	77	78	79	80
81	82	83	84	85	86	87	88	89	90
91	92	93	94	95	96	97	98	99	100

3

1	2	3	4	5	6	7	8	9	10
11	12	13	14	15	16	17	18	19	20
21	22	23	24	25	26	27	28	29	30
31	32	33	34	35	36	37	38	39	40
41	42	43	44	45	46	47	48	49	50

4

51	52	53	54	55	56	57	58	59	60
61	62	63	64	65	66	67	68	69	70
71	72	73	74	75	76	77	78	79	80
81	82	83	84	85	86	87	88	89	90
91	92	93	94	95	96	97	98	99	100

13 Table of Numbers ♦1 to 100

1

1	2	3	4	5	6	7	8	9	10
11	12	13	14	15	16	17	18	19	20
21	22	23	24	25	26	27	28	29	30
31	32	33	34	35	36	37	38	39	40
41	42	43	44	45	46	47	48	49	50

2

51	52	53	54	55	56	57	58	59	60
61	62	63	64	65	66	67	68	69	70
71	72	73	74	75	76	77	78	79	80
81	82	83	84	85	86	87	88	89	90
91	92	93	94	95	96	97	98	99	100

© Kumon Publishing Co., Ltd.

(3)

1	2	3	4	5	6	7	8	9	10
11	12	13	14	15	16	17	18	19	20
21	22	23	24	25	26	27	28	29	30
31	32	33	34	35	36	37	38	39	40
41	42	43	44	45	46	47	48	49	50

(4)

51	52	53	54	55	56	57	58	59	60
61	62	63	64	65	66	67	68	69	70
71	72	73	74	75	76	77	78	79	80
81	82	83	84	85	86	87	88	89	90
91	92	93	94	95	96	97	98	99	100

(14) Table of Numbers ◆To 120 — pp 28, 29

(1)

61	62	63	64	65	66	67	68	69	70
71	72	73	74	75	76	77	78	79	80
81	82	83	84	85	86	87	88	89	90
91	92	93	94	95	96	97	98	99	100
101	102	103	104	105	106	107	108	109	110

(2)

71	72	73	74	75	76	77	78	79	80
81	82	83	84	85	86	87	88	89	90
91	92	93	94	95	96	97	98	99	100
101	102	103	104	105	106	107	108	109	110
111	112	113	114	115	116	117	118	119	120

(3)

61	62	63	64	65	66	67	68	69	70
71	72	73	74	75	76	77	78	79	80
81	82	83	84	85	86	87	88	89	90
91	92	93	94	95	96	97	98	99	100
101	102	103	104	105	106	107	108	109	110

(4)

71	72	73	74	75	76	77	78	79	80
81	82	83	84	85	86	87	88	89	90
91	92	93	94	95	96	97	98	99	100
101	102	103	104	105	106	107	108	109	110
111	112	113	114	115	116	117	118	119	120

(15) Adding 1 ◆1+1 to 10+1 — pp 30, 31

(1)
(1) 2 (6) 5
(2) 3 (7) 6
(3) 4 (8) 8
(4) 5 (9) 10
(5) 7 (10) 9

(2)
(1) 3 (3) 6
    3   6
(2) 4 (4) 7
    4   7

(3) Advice

Could you write the number sentences while reading them aloud? Practice adding 1 some more!

(4)
(1) 5 (7) 5
(2) 6 (8) 7
(3) 7 (9) 8
(4) 2 (10) 9
(5) 3 (11) 10
(6) 4 (12) 11

(16) Adding 1 ◆1+1 to 10+1 — pp 32, 33

(1)
(1) 5 (6) 10
(2) 4 (7) 9
(3) 3 (8) 8
(4) 2 (9) 7
(5) 11 (10) 6

(2)
(1) 2 (6) 5
(2) 4 (7) 7
(3) 6 (8) 9
(4) 8 (9) 11
(5) 3 (10) 10

(3)
(1) 5 (11) 3
(2) 8 (12) 7
(3) 10 (13) 8
(4) 4 (14) 5
(5) 3 (15) 11
(6) 6 (16) 9
(7) 11 (17) 2
(8) 2 (18) 6
(9) 9 (19) 4
(10) 10 (20) 7

(17) Adding 1 ◆5+1 to 20+1 — pp 34, 35

(1)
(1) 7 (6) 12
(2) 8 (7) 13
(3) 9 (8) 14
(4) 10 (9) 15
(5) 11 (10) 16

(2)
(1) 8 (6) 12
(2) 11 (7) 10
(3) 14 (8) 9
(4) 6 (9) 13
(5) 16 (10) 15

(3)
(1) 12 (6) 17
(2) 13 (7) 18
(3) 14 (8) 19
(4) 15 (9) 20
(5) 16 (10) 21

(4)
(1) 19 (6) 12
(2) 17 (7) 14
(3) 21 (8) 20
(4) 18 (9) 15
(5) 13 (10) 16

18 Adding 1 ◆15+1 to 30+1   pp 36, 37

1
(1) 17	(6) 22
(2) 18	(7) 23
(3) 19	(8) 24
(4) 20	(9) 25
(5) 21	(10) 26

2
(1) 18	(6) 23
(2) 16	(7) 19
(3) 21	(8) 24
(4) 25	(9) 26
(5) 20	(10) 22

3
(1) 22	(6) 27
(2) 23	(7) 28
(3) 24	(8) 29
(4) 25	(9) 30
(5) 26	(10) 31

4
(1) 29	(6) 25
(2) 26	(7) 30
(3) 24	(8) 23
(4) 28	(9) 31
(5) 22	(10) 27

19 Adding 1 ◆25+1 to 40+1   pp 38, 39

1
(1) 27	(6) 32
(2) 28	(7) 33
(3) 29	(8) 34
(4) 30	(9) 35
(5) 31	(10) 36

2
(1) 29	(6) 35
(2) 26	(7) 32
(3) 34	(8) 27
(4) 31	(9) 36
(5) 30	(10) 33

3
(1) 32	(6) 37
(2) 33	(7) 38
(3) 34	(8) 39
(4) 35	(9) 40
(5) 36	(10) 41

4
(1) 38	(6) 40
(2) 37	(7) 35
(3) 41	(8) 34
(4) 39	(9) 36
(5) 32	(10) 33

20 Adding 1 ◆To 100+1 and beyond   pp 40, 41

1
(1) 42	(11) 55
(2) 43	(12) 56
(3) 44	(13) 57
(4) 52	(14) 58
(5) 53	(15) 49
(6) 54	(16) 50
(7) 45	(17) 51
(8) 46	(18) 59
(9) 47	(19) 60
(10) 48	(20) 61

2
(1) 67	(11) 97
(2) 68	(12) 98
(3) 69	(13) 99
(4) 77	(14) 100
(5) 78	(15) 102
(6) 79	(16) 101
(7) 87	(17) 109
(8) 88	(18) 111
(9) 89	(19) 110
(10) 90	(20) 119

21 Adding 2 ◆1+2 to 10+2   pp 42, 43

1
(1) 5
(2) 8
(3) 7

2
(1) 3	(5) 7
(2) 6	(6) 4
(3) 8	(7) 9
(4) 5	(8) 10

3 Advice

Could you write the number sentences while reading them aloud? Practice adding 2 some more!

4
(1) 6	(6) 5
(2) 7	(7) 9
(3) 8	(8) 10
(4) 3	(9) 11
(5) 4	(10) 12

22 Adding 2 ◆1+2 to 10+2   pp 44, 45

1
(1) 6	(6) 11
(2) 5	(7) 10
(3) 4	(8) 9
(4) 3	(9) 8
(5) 12	(10) 7

2
(1) 3	(6) 6
(2) 5	(7) 8
(3) 7	(8) 10
(4) 9	(9) 12
(5) 4	(10) 11

3
(1) 6	(11) 4
(2) 9	(12) 8
(3) 11	(13) 9
(4) 5	(14) 6
(5) 4	(15) 12
(6) 7	(16) 10
(7) 12	(17) 3
(8) 3	(18) 7
(9) 10	(19) 5
(10) 11	(20) 8

23 Adding 2 ◆5+2 to 20+2   pp 46, 47

1
(1) 8	(6) 13
(2) 9	(7) 14
(3) 10	(8) 15
(4) 11	(9) 16
(5) 12	(10) 17

2
(1) 7	(6) 13
(2) 8	(7) 15
(3) 12	(8) 17
(4) 14	(9) 11
(5) 10	(10) 16

3
(1) 13	(6) 18
(2) 14	(7) 19
(3) 15	(8) 20
(4) 16	(9) 21
(5) 17	(10) 22

4
(1) 16	(6) 14
(2) 18	(7) 22
(3) 17	(8) 21
(4) 13	(9) 15
(5) 19	(10) 20

24 Adding 2 ♦14+2 to 30+2

1
(1) 18　(6) 23
(2) 19　(7) 24
(3) 20　(8) 25
(4) 21　(9) 26
(5) 22　(10) 27

2
(1) 16　(6) 24
(2) 22　(7) 27
(3) 25　(8) 20
(4) 23　(9) 26
(5) 18　(10) 21

3
(1) 23　(6) 28
(2) 24　(7) 29
(3) 25　(8) 30
(4) 26　(9) 31
(5) 27　(10) 32

4
(1) 29　(6) 32
(2) 27　(7) 24
(3) 26　(8) 22
(4) 28　(9) 25
(5) 30　(10) 31

25 Adding 2 ♦26+2 to 45+2
pp 50,51

1
(1) 28　(6) 33
(2) 29　(7) 34
(3) 30　(8) 35
(4) 31　(9) 36
(5) 32　(10) 37

2
(1) 29　(6) 31
(2) 32　(7) 28
(3) 35　(8) 36
(4) 37　(9) 30
(5) 33　(10) 34

3
(1) 38　(6) 43
(2) 39　(7) 44
(3) 40　(8) 45
(4) 41　(9) 46
(5) 42　(10) 47

4
(1) 37　(6) 45
(2) 42　(7) 43
(3) 47　(8) 38
(4) 44　(9) 46
(5) 40　(10) 41

26 Adding 3 ♦1+3 to 10+3
pp 52,53

1
(1) 5
(2) 7
(3) 9

2
(1) 4　(5) 8
(2) 6　(6) 7
(3) 5　(7) 9
(4) 7　(8) 10

3 Advice

Could you write the number sentences while reading them aloud? Practice adding 3 some more!

4
(1) 7　(6) 6
(2) 8　(7) 10
(3) 9　(8) 11
(4) 4　(9) 12
(5) 5　(10) 13

27 Adding 3 ♦1+3 to 15+3
pp 54,55

1
(1) 4　(6) 7
(2) 6　(7) 9
(3) 8　(8) 11
(4) 10　(9) 13
(5) 5　(10) 12

2
(1) 7　(6) 8
(2) 10　(7) 6
(3) 12　(8) 4
(4) 13　(9) 9
(5) 5　(10) 11

3
(1) 9　(6) 14
(2) 10　(7) 15
(3) 11　(8) 16
(4) 12　(9) 17
(5) 13　(10) 18

4
(1) 10　(6) 15
(2) 13　(7) 11
(3) 16　(8) 8
(4) 14　(9) 18
(5) 17　(10) 12

28 Adding 3 ♦11+3 to 25+3
pp 56,57

1
(1) 14　(6) 19
(2) 15　(7) 20
(3) 16　(8) 21
(4) 17　(9) 22
(5) 18　(10) 23

2
(1) 17　(6) 12
(2) 18　(7) 13
(3) 19　(8) 21
(4) 20　(9) 22
(5) 11　(10) 23

3
(1) 10　(6) 24
(2) 20　(7) 25
(3) 21　(8) 26
(4) 22　(9) 27
(5) 23　(10) 28

4
(1) 17　(6) 28
(2) 27　(7) 20
(3) 14　(8) 21
(4) 24　(9) 25
(5) 26　(10) 22

Advice

Regarding "Adding 1," "Adding 2," and "Adding 3," keep practicing until you can complete the exercises easily and quickly.

29 Adding 4 ♦To 10+4
pp 58,59

1
(1) 2　(11) 6
(2) 3　(12) 7
(3) 4　(13) 8
(4) 5　(14) 9
(5) 5　(15) 5
(6) 6　(16) 6
(7) 7　(17) 7
(8) 8　(18) 8
(9) 4　(19) 9
(10) 5　(20) 10

2 Advice

Was this part easy? Keep practicing!

3
(1) 5　(6) 10
(2) 7　(7) 12
(3) 9　(8) 14
(4) 6　(9) 13
(5) 8　(10) 11

30 Adding 4 ◆To 19+4 pp 60,61

1
(1) 11	(6) 15
(2) 7	(7) 16
(3) 12	(8) 17
(4) 13	(9) 18
(5) 14	(10) 19

2
(1) 13	(6) 9
(2) 7	(7) 19
(3) 17	(8) 12
(4) 15	(9) 10
(5) 16	(10) 18

3
(1) 17	(6) 22
(2) 18	(7) 23
(3) 19	(8) 13
(4) 20	(9) 12
(5) 21	(10) 11

4
(1) 12	(6) 9
(2) 22	(7) 17
(3) 18	(8) 13
(4) 11	(9) 20
(5) 21	(10) 22

31 Adding 5 ◆To 10+5 pp 62,63

1
(1) 4	(11) 7
(2) 5	(12) 6
(3) 6	(13) 7
(4) 5	(14) 8
(5) 6	(15) 9
(6) 7	(16) 10
(7) 8	(17) 8
(8) 9	(18) 9
(9) 5	(19) 10
(10) 6	(20) 11

2 Advice

How did you do? Practice makes perfect!

3
(1) 7	(6) 12
(2) 9	(7) 14
(3) 6	(8) 11
(4) 8	(9) 13
(5) 10	(10) 15

32 Adding 5 ◆To 19+5 pp 64,65

1
(1) 14	(6) 8
(2) 15	(7) 18
(3) 16	(8) 9
(4) 7	(9) 19
(5) 17	(10) 12

2
(1) 10	(6) 17
(2) 13	(7) 12
(3) 16	(8) 15
(4) 11	(9) 18
(5) 14	(10) 19

3
(1) 18	(6) 23
(2) 19	(7) 24
(3) 20	(8) 15
(4) 21	(9) 16
(5) 22	(10) 17

4
(1) 11	(6) 18
(2) 21	(7) 14
(3) 13	(8) 24
(4) 23	(9) 12
(5) 8	(10) 22

33 Adding 6 ◆To 10+6 pp 66,67

1
(1) 4	(11) 8
(2) 5	(12) 9
(3) 6	(13) 10
(4) 7	(14) 11
(5) 7	(15) 7
(6) 8	(16) 8
(7) 9	(17) 9
(8) 10	(18) 10
(9) 6	(19) 11
(10) 7	(20) 12

2
(1) 7	(6) 12
(2) 8	(7) 13
(3) 9	(8) 14
(4) 10	(9) 15
(5) 11	(10) 16

3
(1) 10	(6) 9
(2) 11	(7) 13
(3) 12	(8) 14
(4) 7	(9) 15
(5) 8	(10) 16

34 Adding 6 ◆1+6 to 15+6 pp 68,69

1
(1) 7	(6) 11
(2) 9	(7) 13
(3) 8	(8) 15
(4) 10	(9) 16
(5) 12	(10) 14

2
(1) 16	(6) 21
(2) 17	(7) 9
(3) 18	(8) 19
(4) 19	(9) 10
(5) 20	(10) 20

3
(1) 13	(11) 7
(2) 18	(12) 13
(3) 20	(13) 19
(4) 11	(14) 8
(5) 8	(15) 14
(6) 21	(16) 20
(7) 15	(17) 9
(8) 19	(18) 15
(9) 14	(19) 21
(10) 17	(20) 18

35 Adding 7 ◆To 10+7 pp 70,71

1
(1) 6	(6) 8
(2) 7	(7) 9
(3) 8	(8) 10
(4) 10	(9) 12
(5) 11	(10) 13

2
(1) 8	(6) 13
(2) 9	(7) 14
(3) 10	(8) 15
(4) 11	(9) 16
(5) 12	(10) 17

3
(1) 11	(6) 10
(2) 12	(7) 14
(3) 13	(8) 15
(4) 8	(9) 16
(5) 9	(10) 17

4
(1) 9	(6) 13
(2) 8	(7) 15
(3) 10	(8) 17
(4) 12	(9) 16
(5) 11	(10) 14

36 Adding 7 & 8 pp 72,73

①
(1) 16	(6) 10
(2) 17	(7) 20
(3) 18	(8) 21
(4) 19	(9) 22
(5) 9	(10) 12

②
(1) 12	(6) 22
(2) 18	(7) 16
(3) 15	(8) 21
(4) 20	(9) 17
(5) 11	(10) 10

③
(1) 7	(6) 10
(2) 8	(7) 11
(3) 9	(8) 12
(4) 11	(9) 13
(5) 12	(10) 14

④
(1) 9	(6) 14
(2) 10	(7) 15
(3) 11	(8) 16
(4) 12	(9) 17
(5) 13	(10) 18

37 Adding 8 pp 74,75

①
(1) 12	(6) 11
(2) 13	(7) 15
(3) 14	(8) 16
(4) 9	(9) 17
(5) 10	(10) 18

②
(1) 16	(6) 14
(2) 13	(7) 11
(3) 18	(8) 10
(4) 15	(9) 17
(5) 9	(10) 12

③
(1) 17	(6) 11
(2) 18	(7) 21
(3) 19	(8) 22
(4) 20	(9) 23
(5) 10	(10) 15

④
(1) 15	(6) 11
(2) 21	(7) 9
(3) 13	(8) 19
(4) 22	(9) 12
(5) 17	(10) 23

38 Adding 9 pp 76,77

①
(1) 8	(6) 9
(2) 9	(7) 10
(3) 10	(8) 11
(4) 12	(9) 13
(5) 13	(10) 14

②
(1) 10	(6) 15
(2) 11	(7) 16
(3) 12	(8) 17
(4) 13	(9) 18
(5) 14	(10) 19

③
(1) 12	(6) 13
(2) 17	(7) 18
(3) 14	(8) 11
(4) 10	(9) 19
(5) 16	(10) 15

④
(1) 17	(6) 22
(2) 18	(7) 15
(3) 19	(8) 17
(4) 20	(9) 12
(5) 21	(10) 22

39 Adding 9 & 10 pp 78,79

①
(1) 16	(6) 20
(2) 15	(7) 22
(3) 18	(8) 23
(4) 17	(9) 24
(5) 19	(10) 21

②
(1) 11	(6) 16
(2) 12	(7) 17
(3) 13	(8) 18
(4) 14	(9) 19
(5) 15	(10) 20

③
(1) 18	(6) 23
(2) 14	(7) 14
(3) 19	(8) 24
(4) 16	(9) 17
(5) 21	(10) 20

④
(1) 17	(6) 21
(2) 16	(7) 23
(3) 19	(8) 24
(4) 18	(9) 22
(5) 20	(10) 25

40 Adding ◆Sums up to 16 pp 80,81

①
(1) 9	(14) 11
(2) 14	(15) 14
(3) 11	(16) 15
(4) 16	(17) 13
(5) 11	(18) 12
(6) 15	(19) 16
(7) 13	(20) 14
(8) 15	(21) 12
(9) 13	(22) 16
(10) 16	(23) 14
(11) 14	(24) 16
(12) 11	(25) 16
(13) 13	

②
(1) 14	(14) 14
(2) 15	(15) 16
(3) 15	(16) 16
(4) 15	(17) 16
(5) 16	(18) 13
(6) 16	(19) 13
(7) 15	(20) 16
(8) 15	(21) 14
(9) 16	(22) 15
(10) 16	(23) 15
(11) 15	(24) 16
(12) 14	(25) 16
(13) 14	

41 Adding ◆Sums up to 20 pp 82,83

①
(1) 14	(14) 18
(2) 15	(15) 18
(3) 16	(16) 18
(4) 13	(17) 12
(5) 18	(18) 15
(6) 15	(19) 18
(7) 18	(20) 17
(8) 18	(21) 17
(9) 15	(22) 17
(10) 17	(23) 18
(11) 18	(24) 17
(12) 18	(25) 18
(13) 16	

②
(1) 19	(14) 19
(2) 18	(15) 19
(3) 20	(16) 20
(4) 20	(17) 18
(5) 18	(18) 20
(6) 20	(19) 19
(7) 19	(20) 18
(8) 18	(21) 20
(9) 20	(22) 19
(10) 19	(23) 20
(11) 19	(24) 20
(12) 19	(25) 20
(13) 17	

1
(1)	13	(14)	18
(2)	16	(15)	22
(3)	15	(16)	20
(4)	14	(17)	24
(5)	17	(18)	24
(6)	19	(19)	19
(7)	18	(20)	21
(8)	19	(21)	22
(9)	16	(22)	24
(10)	19	(23)	23
(11)	21	(24)	22
(12)	20	(25)	24
(13)	22		

2
(1)	16	(14)	26
(2)	19	(15)	23
(3)	23	(16)	26
(4)	22	(17)	26
(5)	24	(18)	27
(6)	26	(19)	25
(7)	26	(20)	26
(8)	27	(21)	28
(9)	28	(22)	26
(10)	26	(23)	23
(11)	28	(24)	26
(12)	25	(25)	28
(13)	23		

Advice

If you made many mistakes in **1**, start reviewing on page 2.

If you made many mistakes in **2**, start reviewing on page 30.

If you made many mistakes in **3**, start reviewing on page 66.

If you made many mistakes in **4**, start reviewing on page 80.

43 **Review**   pp 86, 87

1
61	62	63	64	65	66	67	68	69	70
71	72	73	74	75	76	77	78	79	80
81	82	83	84	85	86	87	88	89	90
91	92	93	94	95	96	97	98	99	100

2
(1)	7	(9)	13
(2)	10	(10)	12
(3)	8	(11)	10
(4)	10	(12)	11
(5)	7	(13)	12
(6)	6	(14)	14
(7)	10	(15)	13
(8)	9	(16)	10

3
(1)	9	(7)	10
(2)	11	(8)	14
(3)	13	(9)	17
(4)	11	(10)	16
(5)	13	(11)	14
(6)	15	(12)	17

4
(1)	10	(9)	11
(2)	12	(10)	7
(3)	12	(11)	15
(4)	14	(12)	12
(5)	12	(13)	7
(6)	11	(14)	18
(7)	15	(15)	13
(8)	12	(16)	3